# ELECTION NIGHT
AND THE FIVE SATINS

TIM SUERMONDT

GLASS LYRE PRESS

Copyright © 2016 Tim Suermondt
Paperback ISBN: 978-1-941783-18-4

All rights reserved: except for the purpose of quoting brief passages for review, no part of this book may be reproduced or transmitted in any form or by any means, electronic or mechanical, including photocopying, recording, or by any information storage and retrieval system, without permission in writing from the publisher.

Cover art: Pui Ying Wong
Design & layout: Steven Asmussen
Copyediting: Linda E. Kim
Author photo: Pui Ying Wong

Glass Lyre Press, LLC
P.O. Box 2693
Glenview, IL 60026

www.GlassLyrePress.com

# Contents

| | |
|---|---|
| What a Man Of Simple Means Knows About Paradise | 11 |
| Stanley the Magician | 12 |
| The Great Poet in the Early Days | 13 |
| Jean Moulin | 14 |
| The Philosopher of Basketball | 15 |
| Two Angels Down At Immaculate Heart of Mary Church | 16 |
| Drinking Tea With Shu Qi On a Hotel Balcony in Hanoi | 17 |
| Looking for Zagajewski Under the Couch | 18 |
| Hang Gliding at Delphi | 19 |
| Some Unmentionables in the City of Light | 20 |
| The Usual | 21 |
| Mucho Shoes | 22 |
| Waiting for a Plane to Paris | 23 |
| Jesus Dances the Cha-Cha | 24 |
| For the Haxton Southerners | 25 |
| The Same World | 27 |
| What I Owe Vermeer | 28 |
| The End of Fame | 29 |

| | |
|---|---|
| Christmas on the Subway | 30 |
| Election Night and the Five Satins | 31 |
| A Basketball Hoop in Auvers | 32 |
| Princeton, 1954 | 33 |
| The Beautiful Sheen | 34 |
| Renaldo in Monmartre | 35 |
| The Bandages are Taking a Vacation | 36 |
| 2,000 Cows Get Swept Out to Sea in Puerto Rico | 37 |
| Bill Can Only Stay a Moment | 38 |
| One Last Time | 39 |
| Goodbye Margo | 40 |
| Bluer Moon | 41 |
| Key Food | 42 |
| Charles Dickens at Hotel Rasco | 43 |
| Even if Blue Panties Can't Save a Man | 44 |
| Marriage | 45 |
| There are a Lot of Angels in Poetry, But I Don't Mind | 46 |
| Linen White | 48 |
| Closing the Sky Window | 49 |
| For a Friend Recently Divorced | 50 |
| His Last Poem | 51 |
| Reading About a Supermodel Who Says She Had Sex Swinging From a Tree | 52 |
| Luftmensch | 53 |
| The House of the World | 54 |

| | |
|---|---|
| The Perfect Political Poem | 55 |
| Gratitude at Last | 56 |
| My Old Life | 57 |
| December | 58 |
| Revelation | 59 |
| The Summer Theft | 60 |
| When I Get There, If I Get There | 61 |
| Spring for Certain Men | 62 |
| Odyssey | 63 |
| Little Faith | 64 |
| The Centerfielder will Tell You He's Key | 65 |
| Pilgrimage in Question | 66 |
| I Hear the Voices of My Buddies | 68 |
| The Unemployment Waltz | 69 |
| Lovely Word | 70 |
| Scribbling in Paris | 71 |
| What It's All About | 72 |
| Real Physics | 73 |
| Survival Song | 74 |

| | |
|---|---|
| Acknowledgments | 75 |
| About the Author | 77 |

FOR PUI YING AND IN MEMORY OF EDDIE

We are all in the gutter, but some of us are looking at the stars.

—Oscar Wilde

Too much of a good thing can be simply wonderful.

—Mae West

## What a Man Of Simple Means Knows About Paradise

That you can travel anywhere
and forever,
the woman you love content
to roam in white dresses only.

That poetry there is bread,
butter and jam,
beautiful as cobbler pie,
rugged as a carpenter's hammer—

that it even
has a bowling alley.

# Stanley the Magician

He was lousy—
Not once, during the thousands of times he tried the trick,
did he pull the rabbit out of the hat.
And this was only
his most glaring shortcoming.
Even so, there were people
who came to see him perform
and the Magician's Union held him
in good standing, perhaps attributable
to the mystery
where a man who's the worst at what he does
is often more intriguing
than the man who's the best.

When he died, twenty magicians paid their respects—
one from Sydney, one from Lublin—
They filed past his open coffin,
each one breaking a wand in half
and placing it carefully among the velvet folds
before leaning over to whisper in his ear:
ALACAZAM.
How ideal it would be to report
that, finally, he found the right magic,
how he popped out of the coffin
sharper and more surprised than Lazarus, shouting:
"Bring on the rabbit!"
But we know better.
Then again, as Stanley used to suggest
with unfailing aplomb: Go ahead. Pick a card, any card.

## The Great Poet in the Early Days
for Eddie

Consigned to the cleaning
of the Section 5 and 7 floors
at the Border Air Craft Factory

I carried my mop and pail
like they were pen and pad
and wrote great poems in my head—

if only I'd gotten them on paper
for proof. I washed grease and smudge,
changed them into rivers and cities

that reflected beneath me,
every inch shinier than moonlight
on a clear night, colors so sharp

they would have startled the blind
as well—Oh it was all poor
but romantic, far less lonely

than the mopping I do in my small
apartment, my great poems residing
in a folder now, getting older, steadying

themselves for a move to a simpler town
whose name I too might one day
no longer conjure nor remember.

# Jean Moulin

Our earlier photographs
make us ask
if we were that handsome,
or at least
that better looking
than we are now.
Notice the jauntiness
we display toward
the future, a slightly
silly grin only
because of the camera's time.
We often wrote dates,
names on the back—
and notes "Missing you
much Marie" and the like
as if the photographs
and we ourselves
were indestructible
no matter the shredding,
certain to be showing up
again and again,
astonished and alive,
handsomer than ever.

# The Philosopher of Basketball

As he writes in his study
sunlight pours through the lone window
as if to accentuate
the importance of his work.

He's mixing like a master
the arcane points of the game
with the popular tradition—
he makes a note of 'Fly with Sly'

and the gorgeous moves capable
of crowning a man 'King of French pastry',
all the grit and flash
aiding the living of the ethical life.

Under a chapter heading titled
'Time and the Concept of Swish'
he doodles a basketball
the way a child draws a moon—

skims his fingers over it
as if it were the real thing
"Beautiful to the touch, brothers,
Beautiful to the touch."

# Two Angels Down
## At Immaculate Heart of Mary Church

Around 75 white angels, clustered
about the front and side lawn—

each angel created from stitch wire
and flimsy cloth, each angel

blowing a silver saran trumpet,
each angel carrying the tag:

'In Memory Of"... my favorite,
Otis Meadowlark—one suspects

that any man with such a name
had to have been a decent soul.

This is as close as I will get
to angels, not counting

the imaginary angels I conjure up,
comradely, though not always

for the best of reasons.
I'm tempted to bend, set

the two fallen angels upright—
no, there's a purpose for it (maybe),

and maybe it is better to let
the angels lie in the grass,

face to face like a wondering couple
as a reminder to life and the living.

## Drinking Tea With Shu Qi On a Hotel Balcony in Hanoi

"This tea is wonderful," she says in Cantonese,
rimming her cup with one of her red fingernails.
She looks stunning in her tennis ensemble,
vivid as the flame trees lining the main boulevard.
She's too young to care about an old war and invoking
it would serve to make me absurd, hopelessly out of date.
Better to stick to current restaurants, movies
and the like, keeping our talk modern and thin
as nylon stockings draped over a shower rod
in a tiny room made white by the light
of the moon. "I can't believe we're here, together," she says.
"Imagination's a tricky thing," and I propose a toast
to Lyndon Johnson. "It's not important you know who he is,
but he'd appreciate that toast. He'd appreciate it a lot."

# Looking for Zagajewski Under the Couch

If his book of poems isn't there
it may be lost forever
and the household will be diminished—
a bit like the neighborhood itself.
The sun will shine less,
the wind will blow harder
and there'll be fewer cherry blossoms
on the trees this Spring, flaunting
themselves in the Japanese Garden.

# Hang Gliding at Delphi

From the top of the ancient stadium
the morning is filtered through
the light which follows me step-by-step,
wherever I decide to take it.
Every pilgrim's icon
flames from Thebes to here,
every campsite and hotel
is singed a dirty white
by the heat of August.
All the German tourists
file out of their buses,
filling the air with election talk—
So many serious voices!
The voices, however, inside me
are a good bit more frivolous,
open to the brightest image
throbbing across the highest plain:
A girl without subtlety, without history,
proving that she commands the language of love—
How can my future not turn out well?

I close my eyes
and fly over the twin mountain peaks,
gliding down towards Itea—
A human pelican
trying to rest, to purify himself
in the harbor water.
The lone word on the tip of my tongue
is the loveliest—
CHAIRETE: Goodbye and be happy.
Today it's the only word worth saying,
the only word worth leaving behind.

# Some Unmentionables in the City of Light

I zero in on a pair of green panties
and its bright yellow rugby ball design on the crotch.
"I'd never wear that," Pui says, anticipating my question.

I'm a bit disappointed given my affinity for ball games
of every sort. But I'm proud she attends to the choosing
of her underwear the same seriousness I do my caps—

the ones that scream Jose Reyes, Pedro Martinez
and Willie Mays' last sad year with the Mets.
Pui selects three lovelies ( pink, blue and black )—

she hands them to me and I cup them like I would
a wounded bird. She rests her head on my arm
and says "All the panties in the world are here"

as I lift my hands toward the glass ceiling's light
and watch the panties turn golden. What a woman.
The Liberation of Paris must have felt like this. It must have.

# The Usual

When my barber cuts my hair today
he expands my knowledge of Cuba—
this time dispensing a bit of history
of palm trees, stressing how very much
he misses them. "I am a grown man, Tim,
but I could weep for them. I could weep
for them." After one final snip
he has me squint in the hand mirror:
"You like? Okay?" "Alfredo, it's perfecto
as usual"—which is what I always say.
I pay him the same amount, give him
the same tip, utter the same farewell.
On the street I look around for palm trees.
Of course I don't see any, and a part of me
feels inconsolable. Even pretty women
passing by won't be able to uproot
the loss starting to make itself at home.
I could weep for them too—the palm trees
that is. Well why not? The day is still young.

# Mucho Shoes

The man was clearly crestfallen—
he kept saying "mucho shoes," "mucho shoes"
over and over. As I looked around the big store—
all the shoes, some in boxes, lined in rows

like orphans at their dinner tables
or cramped together in cold metal framed beds,
the palpable melancholy of the place
and its inhabitants hastened my choice:

a semi-work pair, brown, good and cheap—
they fit beautifully, beautifully. I patted
the man on the back and headed for the register—
for an instant I saw shoes rustle in unison,

then the faint "Please, please take us with you."
I had done what I could, and so had the man.
Outside the showers stopped. In my new shoes
I walked the streets, following the fading rainbow home.

# Waiting for a Plane to Paris

I watch a woman
with multi-colored scarves in her hair
walk by and hope a woman in Paris,
with multi-colored scarves in her hair,
is waiting for me,
a woman entangled in nylons in her bed,
a woman I will like if not love.
In a flat in the Marias
chairs hang from a wall,
Ponge lies on a red table, pears and beer
in the refrigerator—so many months
of beautiful anticipation. I'm glad
I know nothing and have everything to learn.

# Jesus Dances the Cha-Cha

The city is perfectly
clear beneath him
and there's not an angel in sight.
He does the steps flawlessly,
a master of the forward and back.
It does seem to give him joy
though his stoic expression
hints at some stubborn sadness.
Ask him and he'd beg off,
insisting he doesn't know
everything and directing
your attention to his blue dancing
shoes: "I hope you like them.
They mean the world to me."

## For the Haxton Southerners

Longing is the word
but it isn't nearly long enough
to constitute a satisfactory definition—
the problem's that
you can't adequately name the sucker
and what's missing stays missing.
Whether you're feeling lighthearted
or heavy as days old hardtack
this unnamable desire
follows you everywhere,
clouding any success
you may have been lucky to salvage.
I've had the notion
of seeing the whole circumstance
like the Army of Northern Virginia
as it crossed the river, leaving Antietam,
leaving behind any realistic hope
of conquering the Yankees—
and of Stonewall Jackson, writing after Manassas:
'The Good Lord
still doesn't mean for us to win'—
the miraculous ease of losing:
a woman, an idea, a South.
You can't measure
what it is I'm after,
beyond some solace, a glimpse of glory
incapable of going wrong.
Joining you, I've put my feet
into both camps

and I'm patrolling the night,
moving through the sorority of lights
on the battlefield
here in the City along the Hudson,
there, there in a deep ravine along the Mississippi.

# The Same World

"It's tough,"
the man with the moustache said,
"the weight of the world."

"That's true," I said,
"but the weight will lessen
if you shave off the moustache."

"Why I'll go do it right now"—
and he meant it.
I thought of the old rabbis

on Clinton Street, hunched
over texts wide as their beards.
Imagine the weight they carried—

a little less hair here, a little
less hair there, means nothing.
"Keep it on," I said,

not to the man who was already
faraway, but to the summer air,
thick as his moustache.

## What I Owe Vermeer

It's the bowl of fruit—
the knife on the table,
handy as an angel in heaven.

It's the woman who saw the light
by stepping out of the shadow, her white
pitcher sturdier now than whalebone.

It's the man hidden outside
the frame, asking for a slice of bread
with butter, asking for forgiveness.

# The End of Fame

It happens every time
the flowers pop-up.

Every time sunlight
slips through the shadows
with the precision
of a jeweler's hands.

Every time a man and woman
( alone or together )
sit down for dinner.

It happens every time
a pigeon pecks at
and shits on the marble
head of the little
Roman boy god
in the Palais Royal.

## Christmas on the Subway

I started reading
and was astonished:
That poem mocking history

must surely have
been written by me—
but no, the credit

goes to a poet
who once was on many
people's lips, but

has now been forgotten.
I felt a little sorry for him
the way I felt

a little sorry for myself.
I'm not embarrassed to admit
that at this stage,

amidst the voices: Spanish,
Chinese and Russian,
I began mumbling 'Amazing Grace'

but, better yet, closed my eyes
and took a nap wherein
I was the one who gave directions

to Bethlehem. I had helped
save the world. Who among us
would have believed it?

## Election Night and the Five Satins

Walking in the early evening
I run into a group of black girls
singing their unique amalgam
of doo-wop and hip hop.
I wonder if the girls
have heard of the Five Satins
or know that two of them
grew up in the neighborhood.
One of the girls recognizes me
and asks if my man
will be the winner. "We'll see"—
it's as far as my optimism allows.
When I get to the apartment
the night is so quiet
you could hear a pin before it drops,
a solitude so robust
I sympathize with the idea
that any tragedy in the world
doesn't matter, so long
as it takes place faraway.
I turn on the TV
and on a split screen
are the two candidates,
each giving his goofy thumbs up.
No, there's no Roosevelt, no Churchill,
no Five Satins for that matter.
On my way to the kitchen
I start singing 'In the still of the night
I held you, held you tight...'
but softly, for the sake of modesty,
for the good of the Republic.

## A Basketball Hoop in Auvers

A shot hangs momentarily
in the air, like an angel
over a cloud, before dropping
through in perfect silence.

It gets the attention
of the painters, spirits
camped in the wheat fields
like Bill Russell in the paint.

"Magnifique," one says.
"Extraordinaire," says another.
"Nothing but Net," they'd all
say, if they knew the term.

## Princeton, 1954

"A red garter for Tubingen,"
Albert Einstein says

as he winds up the mechanical bird,
ignoring Unified Field Theory talk

like fame for another day.
The bird rattles out the open door,

its suction cupped feet
making their way onto the street,

past the white houses,
the magnolia and the dogwood,

down the incline, down Spruce
where a woman new in town

but an old lover of mathematics
brushes her boy's blond hair

and helps him button his coat—
the winter has come early

and the heavens are forever.

# THE BEAUTIFUL SHEEN

There it was: the blue porpoise
lying among the trash on 4th Avenue.
I could picture it splashing
in our inflatable pool, leaping between
high-rises—its beautiful sheen
bright as a beacon light. But for all
my enthusiasm, its slick skin
made carrying it home impossible.
So I brought Pui red roses instead—
she thanked me but in her heart
must have wished I had demonstrated
a more imaginative touch. "I wanted
to bring back a blue porpoise." "Oh honey,"
she said, stroking my cheek, "of course you did."

## Renaldo in Monmartre

He says his feet are revving up,
although he has no regret
about his moving to Paris and living

in a wreck of an apartment almost
the size of a cupcake. "I feel
luck in my heart when I arrive

and I feel luck in my heart
when I return." He says he's going
home to Juarez to see baseball

on TV, his beloved Dodgers in particular.
He says he's going to tell
his wife, who left him one evening for good,

how foolish she was to complain
whenever he mentioned Chico Ruiz,
Senor Smoke and the great Vada Pinson.

"Some people they never understand
how hard it is to hit
the splitter. You must forgive them."

# THE BANDAGES ARE TAKING A VACATION
## after Mandelstam

They unwrap themselves from the soldiers,
the women, the children in their houses
and the orphanage.
They unwrap themselves from the entire city,
even from the sky
they shrouded completely in white.
They commandeer the trains and buses,
airplanes, a bicycle here and there
for the more adventurous.
They head West, East, North and South,
wave for the delicious sake of waving,
promising "We'll be back."

# 2,000 Cows Get Swept Out to Sea in Puerto Rico
for William Kennedy

And the people on the beach
are realizing that these are

no longer merely dumb beasts.
The cows affect a brave calm,

their heads steady above
the water, regal in profile.

In fact, a girl draws in the sand
a cow with a crown.

A boy asks his father:
"Are the cows going to Miami?"

and the father answers:
"Somewhere. It doesn't matter."

And everyone watches until
the last cow's head disappears

in the distance and a light
from somewhere pink as a tongue.

## Bill Can Only Stay a Moment

I don't pester him with questions:
"So what's the composition of heaven
or whatever place you're at?"
And despite being high on the scale

of importance I don't ask him
why the Mets can't display any heart
on the road—I don't even mention
my frustration at the dive

my hedge fund has taken
as I take him across the Brooklyn
Bridge and point to the Manhattan
side where a schoolyard used to be,

where we played hoops, trying to craft
shots that would gracefully fall through
the bent rims—he was the better
athlete and I tell him.

He lowers his head, watches the sun
dip its glared feet into the river
and insists his repertoire isn't flawless
but he has eternity to make it perfect.

I can't imagine anything better—
and whatever fear and apprehension I have
disappears. "I'm glad I came back,"
he says. I'm glad I made it possible.

# One Last Time

My father loves The Blue Angel
more than Marlene Dietrich—
and how he loves Marlene Dietrich.
We sit in old family chairs
and I watch him as much as the film,
keeping an eye on his advanced age.
He doesn't snooze once, concentrates
throughout like the Intelligence Officer
he was, and at the film's end
says: "That's why I like The Blue Angel.
It's like life—it doesn't end well."
And he smiles, something he so seldom
does I can't remember when he did it before.
I walk him to bed, tuck the blanket
around him. It defies logic, but his
face seems to be getting younger—
could a world long gone be coming
alive one last time, for an instant?
I turn off the light, leave the door
shut halfway. The winter night's still
young. What do I do now?

# Goodbye Margo

It's your mother's last day.

Still you have the courage not to say
"I remember when you cried lovingly onto

my shoulder," or some similar nonsense.
You lift her small body off the couch

and both of you twirl around and around
her small living room. You tell her

of the night, due to the play of light,
she resembled Edgar Allan Poe, and you

promise her had you been in Baltimore then
you'd have pulled him out of the gutter,

done for him what you could. Your mother
lights up like she hasn't in years.

"Truly whacky, but considerate. That's my boy."
The more you twirl the smaller she gets

until she disappears completely out of your arms.
You step onto her small porch and there

she is flying across the sky, waving
ever so strongly. You wave back, then go inside,

sit on the couch, light one of her cigarettes,
watch the smoke snake and dance to the ceiling

and you thank god you were ninety percent stoic
at the end, making your mother, and yourself,

infinitely proud.

# Bluer Moon

I don't know where it's coming from,
but it's a wonderful blues,
that is: lyrics sounding so hopeless
it fills you with joy
because you survived the complaint
the words sing about—you'll live
to see the dogwood bloom again,
live to remember the sad sight
of railroad tracks going nowhere
and marvel at the resiliency of people
love has bruised or passed by—or both.
One night while taking out the trash
you might say to your neighbor:
"I love the blues," and have him respond
"I'm fine too." You'd expect nothing less.

# Key Food
### after Louis Simpson

"It's good to be back,"
I said to the checkout girl.
"I've been working on a long poem."
"That'll be twenty-six dollars,"
she said, "and twenty-two cents."

## Charles Dickens at Hotel Rasco

The sun gets around to shining
like American cheese, yet

I still feel I'm leaving him behind,
just as surely as Tiny Tim

leaves his crutch against the wall
forever. I want to re-establish

the connection between the blister
and the beautiful, appreciate again

Dickens' immense humanity—
and for an instant, eating breakfast

at a diner bordered on both sides
by strip joints, I come close.

A shame it couldn't last
and I'm back to roaming the hills,

the boulevards and side streets,
the slush smeared docks along

the St. Lawrence in mid March—
and even the crows of Montreal

seem to shun any desire to soar.
Hanging on will require a resolve

I may not have, but it's wonderful
to hear his voice powerfully poised

in its own version of loneliness:
"Hello, hello. I'm here to say Goodbye."

# Even if Blue Panties Can't Save a Man

She left in a hurry—
left behind her sheer, blue panties.
A gentleman, I put them in a drawer.

Yesterday
I lost my job, lost my goldfish
and on the other side of the globe

another atrocity was starting up.

It all felt so hopeless
until I remembered the blue panties—

I spread them on the dresser top
and touched the crotch area,
my fingertips feeling more delicate

than the panties—
she was worth it. I wanted to take a walk

and disappear into the blue, ringing a bell—

but I thought better of it and walked
empty-handed,
my steps aping the swagger of a rich man

who has all the lovers and luck
he'll ever need. Some feat.

# Marriage

I've forgotten who gets credit,
inexcusable, but I assure her
I still enjoy
the fine line I remember:
'It's easy to be complex,
hard to be simple.'

"Well," she whispers,
"no one's more complex than me
and no one's simpler than you."
I'm about to say
"That's nice of you"
or some such inanity

When she switches the light off
and starts to undress.
I fiddle with my shirt buttons
only to find every knob stuck.
What if I can't get free?
What if my clothes
become permanently grafted?

And just where do these
strange ideas of mine come from?
Out of the darkness
I feel her knee on my leg,
her hands on my chest.
"Here, let me help you with that.
You and your simplicity."

## There are a Lot of Angels in Poetry, But I Don't Mind

In fact, last week
at the Star Bright Diner
I had lunch with one—
a female dressed
in her satin-white robe,
her gray wings folded

neatly behind her back.
We engaged in small talk—
like friends who had run
into each other on the street.
I did mention my dislike
of the Mayor who's become

a tyrant. "When he shakes
off his mortal coil" she said,
"we'll take care of him"—
what a lovely creature.
I swung for the bill,
kissed her hand

and she flew through the roof—
graceful in her lift-off.
I strolled Times Square,
stopping to gaze at
a huge billboard of a woman
clad for danger, holding

a bottle of men's cologne.
A BIT OF HEAVEN
IN EVERY BOTTLE—
and for the briefest moment
I believed, believed
it was probably true.

# Linen White

I attacked the bathroom,
getting, miraculously, more paint
on the walls than on myself—
so deft were my brushstrokes
that, for an instant, I believed
I might have missed my calling,
been another Vermeer.
Then I remembered the joke
'It is a small world,
but I wouldn't want to paint it'
and concluded my self-congratulation
was mocking me. Enough painting.
I washed up, stepped out
to a darkening afternoon,
walked down Majestic and Warsaw,
thinking of a single shaft of light—
beautiful, beautiful Delft.

## Closing the Sky Window

I love that Chinese expression
about marriage, and its cautionary tone.
But caution will be the last thing

on my mind when I'm at the reception,
stuffing myself with potato salad,
watching my bride get all the attention,

as she should—when I sneak out
and get a glimpse of a tourist boat
shuttling past the Brooklyn Bridge, believing

those who are waving are waving to me—
when I wrap my arms around
my hours old wife and start dancing

so badly she calls it beautiful,
and tells me she's more certain than ever
that both of us are everlasting.

# For a Friend Recently Divorced

The first time you reach out
and feel only the wind,

put your hand in your pant's pocket,
pull out the quarters

and buy the couple of tabloids
you can still enjoy reading alone,

especially given the headlines:
WORLD AT PEACE. AT LAST.

I'm serious. You know anything
is possible, and always did.

# His Last Poem

Written some 30 years from now
just as the sun sets over
the Rappahannock and over

the front porch of the Mary Crystal
Senior Center.

Written just before the nurse
brings him his yogurt, asks
if he'd like a thicker blanket.

Written to a woman who's glad
to be with him again, glad for

immortality if only for a fraction
of time,

glad to be the great force of his
last poem, standing on her toes to show
him the beautiful bass she caught.

## Reading About a Supermodel Who Says She Had Sex Swinging From a Tree

Sounds somewhat enticing
in a bizarre sort of way,
but there's no tree
in the backyard
tall enough, sturdy enough
to allow my girlfriend
and I to give it a try.
"We can grow a tree,"
she says—we can
but by the time
the tree is ready
for such august activity
we'll most likely
find ourselves under it.
"Then let's get naked,"
she says surprisingly
shyly, "and thrash
around in the shower."
Thrash around—so apt,
so poetic, so unlike
the poorer supermodel
who will never blush
in amazement at anything.

## Luftmensch

That's what his family called him,
hoping to shame him into being practical.
They couldn't know
that he was a classic hopeless case,
couldn't know
they'd have an easier time
resurrecting the Kings of old Kiev
than getting him to change.
When the worst happened
and took his family away,
he slipped by, barely noticed,
like a miracle unaware of its gift.
He kept moving,
showing up anywhere, at any time.
He could be in your neighborhood right now,
walking the streets a happy man,
talking about the impossible
and all its beautiful rubbish.

# The House of the World

Doesn't hold the entirety—it only wants to.
As you might have guessed, books predominate—
a Titanic here, a Sputnik there,
a woman weeping in a war zone,
a man marching in Philadelphia, Mississippi—
the life and times of the philosophers
and the history of words themselves,
endless, endless. "A Paradise," as Borges put it—
Jorge Luis who's included on the shelves,
a slim volume of stories tucked between 'Mementos'
and 'Trying to Help the Elephant Man Dance.'

## The Perfect Political Poem

Doesn't want anything to do with politics.
Even if you tortured it, it wouldn't give in.
It would dream of dinner plates,
A pizzeria under the stars, a small river
Running through the middle of the city,
And everything else that's indispensable, period.

## Gratitude at Last

For a very long time
I believed I was meant for greatness.

Don't be too hard on me.
It's part of life: the finally

Growing up and getting the wisdom
To realize that greatness is always

Seeing someone else, that it has
No desire to give me the time of day,

Or night. Really though, I've come
To terms with the miscalculations of my youth.

Eating a croissant that turns golden
In the Paris sun is reason enough

To give thanks for, and when I fish
Along the Canal St-Martin, Hemingway,

His beard broad as Cuba, is always sitting
Beside me, a sparkle in his eyes

Despite the sadness—despite the sadness.
I'm a very fortunate man.

# My Old Life

It had its virtues—
foremost among them
providing me a regular haven
to hide and recover
from the frustrations,
the manifold despairs of life.

My old life is sad
at my leaving, for which
I accept full responsibility—

but I can see my new life
in a fancy car at the curb,
waiting for me to hop in,
drive me to places
I never thought I'd reach.

My new life looks so enticing
I forget to take the suitcase
with the one lonely sticker,
kiss my old life
when I say goodbye.

# December

The snow hauls
its whiteness down the steps
and I regret
not having thrown the shovel
away and escaping
to a land of harsh sun.
I miss the scorched birds,
the blouses melting
in the dead wind,
the water jug starting to glow
in my grateful hands.

# Revelation

Some mystics believe
that in order to create our big world
God had to make himself small.

This is on my mind
as I watch a cop chase a miscreant
who keeps yelling : "I didn't do anything!"—

watch as they become dot-like
and disappear. Small, smaller,
smallest, infinite. I buy a paper,

a man finishes his pastrami on rye,
a woman smoothes wrinkles on her skirt—
it's a happier day, don't complain.

# The Summer Theft

> *En la noche entraremos*
> *a robar*
> *una rama florida.*
> —Pablo Neruda

Easier written than done,
though I'm game
to try and steal a branch
from the apple tree, tonight,
in our neighbor's yard.

But, darling, I no longer climb
fences with the best agility—
you'll have to will
me over by your bootstraps.

And you hold the flashlight—
light the way, light the way.
And if our neighbor,
the old buzzard, should keep
us from completing the mission
by yelling at our shadow
"Who the hell's there!"

we'll retreat, only to return
another night and relieve him
of his satellite dish
which we'll use to signal
the heavens—me on the roof,

in my shabby flip-flops—
and you, darling,
in your red bikini
more beautiful than the stars.

# When I Get There, If I Get There

*Tell me the story of your heart.*
*Does it include a donkey?*
—Maurice Manning

I'm not completely sure about a donkey,
although any type of ass in my poems
is an ass that probably belongs in them.
I wouldn't mind if everything I am
and desire to become rides on the back
of a donkey, its silver bell around its neck
tinkling away as both of us grind up
the steep mountain to the monastery where
the monks have never spoken a word.
When I get there, if I get there, then I'll
start writing the story of my heart, but not
until I've given the donkey water, a bucket
of oats—we made it, old friend, rest now,
rest. We still have a lot of traveling to do.

# Spring for Certain Men

An avenue of women,
all of whom claim they know you
from somewhere, all of whom
call you adorable.

Or to put it another way:

A harsh world, a little
less harsh every day.
The kind of days capable
of making Adorno reconsider—

and there he is:
sitting on a chair in the sky,
like a god or Mozart, writing
his apology, while your father
stays on the narrow front
porch, oiling your baseball glove
as if it were his own.

# Odyssey

Tonight I'll dream of women
bearing gifts—the Greeks
of Union Turnpike who

possess the prestidigitation
to obliterate sadness
by their presence alone.

When I awake
I'll be older. I won't
remember the women—

the alarm clock
holds no magic and my
courage will fail,

my shoes parked nearby—
familiarity: the long ship
that never leaves home.

## Little Faith

The bakery rises in the midday sun—
the croissants alone break through the walls
and spill onto the street.
People arrive with forks and knives
to carve out pieces and carry them home.
Heaven on earth—and you always believed
it wasn't possible.

## The Centerfielder will Tell You He's Key

And once he picks up the white speck
in the early evening sky he knows
he can relax and wait for the ball
to nestle in his glove. Time enough

to remember packing the old rambler
and driving to Galveston—the heat, the lizards,
the oil derricks, and the bars where under
bulbs hung like small moons the locals

talk their baseball—serious philosophers
discussing the roots of happiness, disappointment,
statistics and the imagination indistinguishable—
the city sores healing quicker,

beautiful in memory after all. He drifts
ever so slightly, his throwing hand on his heart
for a tad of showboating, for Willie Mays
who might be watching somewhere in the shadows,

still slick as a basket catch—and for every father
with his impassioned plea to his son: "Don't stand
on a dime." The world that keeps changing, changing,
is once again the same: Inning ending. Threat over.

## Pilgrimage in Question

A good friend is off to Alaska.
He insists he's going nowhere near Juneau

or Anchorage. It's the fierce wilderness
for him, all his commiserations reserved

for the black bears, wolves and coyotes,
the monster whales he calls hunchback.

If everything goes well he'll be
another John Muir discovering another

Glacier Bay, new ice caves and pink alfas
few human beings have ever seen.

If everything goes well I won't hear from
or see him again. Where did he find

the courage and the gall to run away
from Technology and Commerce?

What was it that turned him against
the spirit of Frederick Taylor, Adam Smith?

Like Oscar Wilde, give me the luxuries of life
and I too can do without

the necessities. But one evening
I'll make my sacrifice, turn off the TV,

unplug the computer and go out into
the purple plum night. Under the stars

I'll do a little sea lion dance and invoke
an Eskimo saying: 'The rat race

is over—the rats won.' My friend would be pleased
and tomorrow I can get back to Business.

# I Hear the Voices of My Buddies

Especially as darkness sets in
and the fireflies show up.
My buddies never talk about
the afterlife—I reckon
there's a prohibition against it
or it's a case of them not wanting
to spoil the mystery,
the good and the bad.
But how they reminisce with me
about the previous incarnation,
those strange names again
on everyone's lips: Phu Phong,
Dak Ha, Song Cau, Mo Duc,
Bao Vinh, K Bang...
and when one night I rub my eyes
a shade before midnight
I see a wedding couple
heading for Da Lat, and my buddies—
young as I remember them—
providing escort, dying for R&R
in "La Petite Paris." They turn
and wave and I wave back.
I notice the road widening
to accommodate the lotus blossoms
raining red as tracers. "I'm coming,"
I say ."Wait for me—wait for me."

# The Unemployment Waltz

"C'mon," Unemployment says,
"we haven't danced together in a long time"—
never more true as I struggle
across the courtyard, apologizing for my ungainly steps.
"Relax," Unemployment says, "patience is my art."
A half hour later along the boulevard
I feel progress being made, my feet actually starting
to blossom with every crucial turn—
"I'm going to be rich," I call to a group
of construction workers passing around baloney sandwiches
for lunch, prompting Unemployment to say:
"Balance, Tim, balance. There's only so much I can offer."

# Lovely Word

Now and then, for no reason
that can be justified by reason,
my mind wanders to a baseball park—
the day is always cloudless
with a light that makes
the sluggers bats spark
and the pitches pray for compassion.
I stare straight out beyond
the flagpole to the city's rim
where I imagine a man too
is scratching his head over life,
questions that overwhelm any answers—
my compatriot in confusion
I'd recognize if we ever actually met:
the friendly wave executed
while slightly back on his heels
like a center fielder, albeit the clumsier
variety, drifting back toward the ball,
drifting in the bald hope of success,
drifting, that lovely, lovely word.

## Scribbling in Paris

I'm slumping like the Mets,
but it's early May and we will
( we hope ) come out of it.
To cheer me, my friend,
Henri, expounds on the un-
productive nature of worry:
"Everything," he says, "exists
for a reason and for no reason."
And to buck me up further
my fiancée tells me
the city showers suit me well
like the splendid rain sweepers,
that I'm getting handsomer here
by the day, looking
more and more like Alain Delon—
good god: How many
people still remember him?

# What It's All About
## for Kelly Groucutt

Slightly buzzed, but still civilized,
I bid my friends goodnight

and tramp the crowded streets.
A dance club fused with red lights

rattles out 'Sweet Talking Woman'—
a fond retro beauty. Three well

dressed women, arms locked, exit
and blow me kisses as they antelope

across the avenue. I hum the song
down the stairs to the subway,

waiting for the train to arrive
like a new world. Damn, it's beautiful.

An even older song goes: "Mr. Pies,
no one dies"—and on this kind

of night you can take it to heart
that it's true, the candle immune

to flameout, the time when getting
home is at last worth getting home.

# Real Physics

What the galaxies aspire to
may be less important than we realize—
whatever the galaxies do we have to go
along no matter—Red Giants, White
Dwarfs tenacious in their predictability.
It may be more important
what we aspire to, as we eat our lunch,
terribly in love, our minds already
on the future—all the days to come,
and all the nights too, as we locate
every galaxy by starlight, carried along
with a very, very adaptable wonder.

# Survival Song

Let the cherry blossoms bloom—
I've been in hibernation too long
to wait any longer.
Let me run down the stairs
and hit the street singing.
I sing like a wounded fish
but let the neighbors forgive me—
Let the injustices of the world
beat a momentary retreat
for this reason, this reason alone.
Let the victims know I'm with them
by not insisting I have
a holy bone in my body.
Let Good Friday be damn good—
Let me embrace the first person
who calls me irresponsible.

# Acknowledgments

2 Bridges Review

Able Muse

Amoskeag

Cavalier Literary Couture

Chautauqua Literary Journal

Chiron Review

Cider Press Review

Clapboard House

Concho River Review

Connecticut River Review

Connotation Press (Congeries)

Constellations

Illuminations

Indiana Review

Kestrel

Main Street Rag

Mipoesias

Mudlark

New South

New York Quarterly

Oak Bend Review

Oasis

Olentangy Review

Owen Wister Review

PANK

Paddlefish

Penumbra

Plume Poetry Journal

Poet & Critic

Poetry East

Poetry Storehouse

Prime Mincer

Ray's Road Review

Red Fez

Red River Review

River Styx

| | |
|---|---|
| Rosebud | Tygerburning Literary Journal |
| Stand Magazine (England) | U.S.1 Worksheets |
| Sunstone | Up the Staircase Quarterly |
| The Aurorean | White Pelican Review |
| The Ledge | Wilderness House Literary Review |
| The New Laurel Review | Willows Wept Review |
| Theodate | Zone 3 |

# ABOUT THE AUTHOR

**Tim Suermondt** is the author of two full-length collections of poems: *Trying To Help The Elephant Man Dance* (The Backwaters Press, 2007) and *Just Beautiful* (New York Quarterly Books, 2010)—along with three chapbooks. He has poems published in *Poetry, The Georgia Review, Ploughshares, Prairie Schooner, Blackbird, Bellevue Literary Review, North Dakota Quarterly, december Magazine, Plume Poetry Journal, The Southeast Review, Poetry East,* and *Pirene's Fountain,* among others. He is a book reviewer for Cervena Barva Press and a poetry reviewer for *Bellevue Literary Review*. He lives in Cambridge (MA) with his wife, the poet Pui Ying Wong.

## Glass Lyre Press

exceptional works to replenish the spirit

Glass Lyre Press is an independent literary publisher interested in technically accomplished, stylistically distinct, and original work. Glass Lyre seeks diverse writers that possess a dynamic aesthetic and an ability to emotionally and intellectually engage a wide audience of readers.

Glass Lyre's vision is to connect the world through language and art. We hope to expand the scope of poetry and short fiction for the general reader through exceptionally well-written books, which evoke emotion, provide insight, and resonate with the human spirit.

Poetry Collections
Poetry Chapbooks
Select Short & Flash Fiction
Anthologies

www.GlassLyrePress.com

www.ingramcontent.com/pod-product-compliance
Lightning Source LLC
Chambersburg PA
CBHW021158080526
44588CB00008B/393